ZAFTIG

ZAFTIG

MOLLY ZIPORA PERSHIN FEIGELE RAYNOR

Fifth Avenue Press is a locally focused and publicly owned publishing imprint of the Ann Arbor District Library. It is dedicated to supporting the local writing community by promoting the production of original fiction, nonfiction, and poetry written for children, teens, and adults.

Printed in the United States of America

First Printing 2024

Book Design: Nathaniel Roy
Editor: Zilka Joseph

ISBN: 978-1-956697-27-8 (Paperback)

Fifth Avenue Press
343 S. Fifth Ave
Ann Arbor, MI 48104
fifthavenue.press

For my Great Grandma Dinah, the story we never stop telling

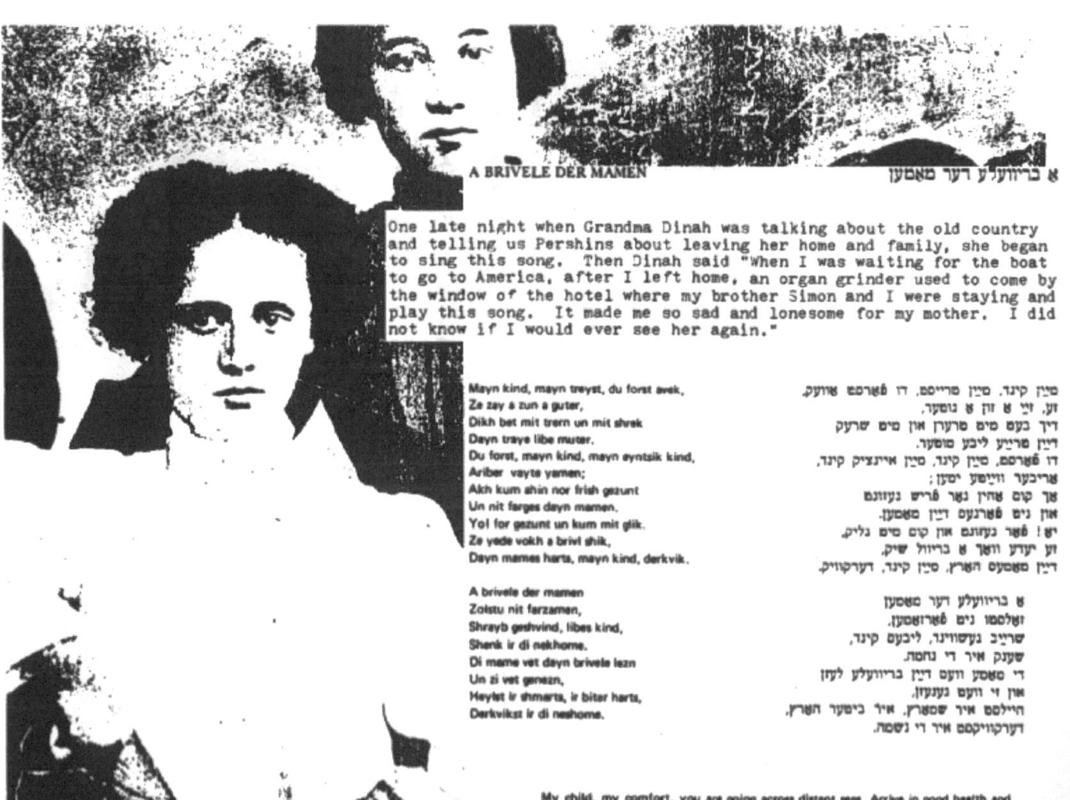

& for Grandy,

the root of my

w i l d

zaf•tig

Origin*

adjective

1. 1930s: Yiddish, from German *saftig* 'juicy'
2. having a full, rounded figure; <u>plump</u> (typically used of a woman).
   "a zaftig brunette"

3. To take up 

*Definition from Oxford Languages Dictionary

CONTENTS

FOREWORD 9

I COME FROM WOMEN WHO MADE LOVE 14

I. KNEADING **15**

ZAFTIG 17

GRANDY, 1939 18

A DRESSED UP POTATO IS STILL A POTATO (YIDDISH PROVERB) 20

AT MY CENTER 22

PREPARING FOR PESACH DURING A PANDEMIC 23

II. BRAIDING **27**

THIS IS THE UNDONE SEASON 28

FEIGELE 29

TOO MUCH [ZAFTIG II] 30

YOU KNOW YOU'VE GOT COVID BRAIN 34

ON FLYING 35

MOVING BACK TO THE CITY WHERE I WAS FIRST RAPED 36

III. RISING **39**

GRANDY, 1990 40

SISTERCHURCH 42

GRANDY, 2002 44

APRIL 2020: BRING ME WATER FOR THESE FLOWERS GROWING OUT MY MIND 46

YAMIM NORAIM /// DAYS OF   A   W   E 48

LABOR 49

ZAFTIG III 50

ACKNOWLEDGMENTS 53

GRATITUDE 55

LAND & LABOR ACKNOWLEDGMENT 57

ABOUT THE AUTHOR 59

FOREWORD
Yalie Saweda Kamara, author of *BESAYDOO*

It's time to celebrate the arrival of Molly Raynor's *ZAFTIG*.

It's time we discuss Raynor's rare and distinct craft. In the span of a little over thirty pages, Raynor resoundingly declares her poetics, which are equally invested in virtuosity, reflection, imagination, and world making—a unique and striking combination.

In *ZAFTIG*'s pages we: smell magnolia, daylilies, roses; hear prayer, Billie Holiday, Lil' Wayne, and the ghosts of foremothers; we see candles flicker, the soul deep gaze of lovers, and the bloodorange sky; we taste sugar cubes, chicken fricassee, and ginger rum; we feel the suppleness of breasts and hips, the winds of Russia, Lake Michigan, and the Pacific Ocean— we are immersed in the visceral, the fragrant, and the complex. While ranging in themes, Raynor's poems possess the singular power to shine and sing, as either an act of praising a perfect moment or triumphantly rising from the tatters of devastation.

Throughout this collection, we see the importance of form, how Raynor's words swim, undulate, expand, refract, swell on, and consume, the page. These choices are intentional, metaphorizing the content of the ideas explored in *ZAFTIG*. Here, Raynor challenges the conventional uses of text. With such compelling skill, we, the readers begin to see anew and the possibilities of language are amplified—who are we to say that a stanza, a line, or a word cannot be the makings of a vegetable, a dress, or a consciousness found in *"A DRESSED UP POTATO IS STILL A POTATO"*? We see these same elements used to embody the emotional turbulence of the trauma endured from sexual assault and the ultimate redemption articulated in *"MOVING BACK TO THE CITY WHERE I WAS FIRST RAPED."* But it isn't just about the placement of words on the page, the resonance of these poems also speaks to the very soul of the words that constitute each of the stories that inhabit *ZAFTIG*. When you really think about it, Raynor's craft begs a one-word question, steeped in a well-earned awe: How?

Part of this "how" may be tied to Raynor's ability to sustain the exploration of stories that populate her world. Ever the archivist and curator, Raynor scrutinizes forgotten and obscured worlds and histories with patience and appreciation. In the wake of *ZAFTIG*'s creation, no ancestor is without a name, matrilineality (which Microsoft Word is currently marking as misspelled) is revered:
dinya
        asna
               dinah
                    fanny
                         betty
                              evie
                                    freda
                                        lois
                                            laura

Tales of suffering, desire, and dreams are resurrected in a bid to learn, to recount, and to honor the strength of bloodlines and survivance. This is found in the black and white and color photos of kin, Grandy's rouged lips that kiss the pages of this collection, the sacred songs and entries in which the currents of Hebrew, Yiddish, and English flow into a wild river, a language of exile, difference, and the yearning to find home, and in the impossibility of this, the creation of a new home. This however, should not be mistaken for the extent of Raynor's project of recovery—there are accounts of the joy and safety that arise from family tradition rooted in choice over circumstance—like the magic of trips to Muskegon in "*AT MY CENTER*" and tradition rooted in humor as seen in "*GRANDY, 1990*"— "Poppa the trickster. Sneaks the raisins from/ her Raisin Bran one by one until /she becomes enraged and calls the /company to complain." We also come to know that home is in who we choose to be ours—this cosmic, intuitive, spiritual and true connection that lovingly complicates and expands notions of family, is so clearly rendered in "*SISTERCHURCH.*" *ZAFTIG* also declares that home is found within the sanctity of self and the resistance of strictures.

In both "*TOO MUCH [ZAFTIG II]*" and "*FEIGELE*" Raynor examines the expectations of a world that privileges misogyny and heteronormativity, observing their threats to dismantle both her identity and agency. While these poems echo painful realities faced by marginalized communities, they also mark these injustices with the indelibility of written witness, documenting societal shortcomings with such passion and exactitude that they become a sort of gauge between who we are and how much work is left to do to heal—to dignify, hold, and see each other. Lucky for us, Raynor offers a solution: explode the world with a fierce beauty and survivance:

 i ursula

             monsterqueen of

   ocean & oyster   pearl & coral

tentacles & naked breasts spilling

over every

surface

splayed across   my golden sheets

   starfish

       suctioned   to   reef

          owned   by no man

but the   sea

                          in my tomorrowland

            i only smile

for me

Moving and gliding across the page, with nary a concern for neatness, Raynor upholds
an allegiance to collapsing borders, psyches, mores, and constitutions: Raynor imagines
to rebirth. To infinity.

It's time to celebrate a collection that is huge.   Limitless.   Big.   Rebelliously
and righteously thick.

          Too, too much *ZAFTIG*, which might really mean that it is just enough.

You remember thinking while braiding your hair that you look a lot like your mother and her mother before her.
It was their whispers that pushed you, their murmurs over pots sizzling in your head.
A thousand women urging you to speak through the blunt tip of your pencil.
Kitchen poets, you call them.

—EDWIDGE DANTICAT

There's a custom tied to a spiritual belief in Judaism
that if forty women bake challah with someone in mind,
it has the power to change the course of natural events.

A segulah.

—LEIGH SHULMAN

I COME FROM
WOMEN WHO MADE LOVE

work. Who made a meal out of need. My
great grandmothers kibitzing in Dinah's hot
kitchen, oiled knuckles caked in fine flour.
I imagine their ghosts gossiping above me,
hovering even in death, making sure I clear
my plate- brisket tender as a widow in grief,
lemon cake tart & dusted in powdered sugar.
They poured faith into the glass of my young
eyes, glinting green & certain. Each with a man
that stuck, waxy & scarlet as their lips on my
cheek, anointing me with gentle warnings &
measurements for the perfect chicken soup.
I cook for two or four, as if my body was wired
to rise like egg-kissed dough, to raise more than
myself. But there is only one. So many leftovers
I take to friends, students. Maybe I was made to
feed other's children. Maybe they are my children
too. Maybe there is no man who will love me as
thick as they do. I come from women who made
love work. Maybe I am a woman who makes work

love. Still, on the eve of my 36th birthday, I hunger
more. I burn a tall red candle, dripping like owed
blood & think about legacy. What I will leave.
What has left me. How the women stay, even
after death. How the men go easy, even while
alive. I have mastered this language of loss,
this recipe of red onion & chili, weeping late
night in my hot kitchen. But I am fluent in other
tongues too: the flame that burns for eight nights
on only enough oil for one. Some days, I am
startled by my own dumb light. How I flicker
blue with bright desire after such ghosting.
Women are not afraid of work & I am not afraid
of love, no matter how much salt stains the pillow.
How much sugar misses the bowl. I am slow &
steady, challah thickening on the windowsill.
I will enter my shadow with silver hairs & sing
my own name until I summon my unsuffering,
until I learn the correct measurements for one.

KNEADING

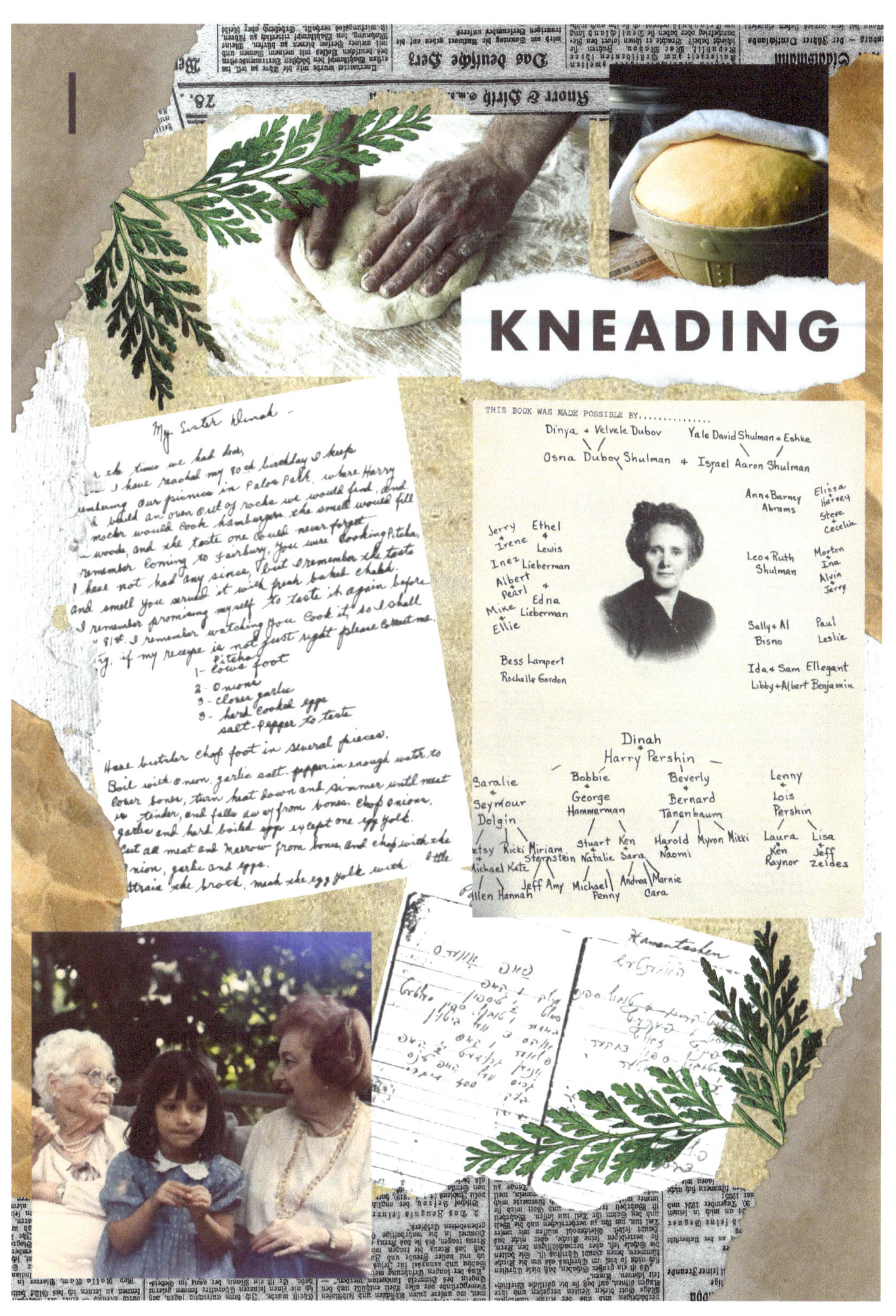
My Sister Dinah —

... the time we had dear,
... I have reached my 80th birthday I keep
remembering our picnics in Palos Park, where Harry
& would build an oven out of rocks we would find, and
mother would cook hamburgers, the smell would fill
in woods, and the taste one could never forget.
remember coming to Fairbury, you were cooking Pitcha,
I have not had any since, but I remember the taste
and smell you served it with fresh baked challah.
I remember promising myself to taste it again before
"81st. I remember watching you cook it, so I shall
try, if my recipe is not just right please correct me.
              Pitcha
       1 - cows foot
       2 - Onion
       3 - cloves garlic
       3 - hard cooked eggs
           salt-pepper to taste

Have butcher chop foot in several pieces.
Boil with onion, garlic, salt-pepper in enough water to
cover bones, turn heat down and simmer until meat
is tender, and falls away from bones. Chop onion,
garlic and hard boiled eggs except one egg yolk.
Cut all meat and marrow from bones and chop with the
onion, garlic and eggs.
Strain the broth, mash the egg yolk with little

THIS BOOK WAS MADE POSSIBLE BY...............

Dinya + Velvele Dubov   Yale David Shulman + Eshke
    Osna Dubov Shulman + Israel Aaron Shulman

                                    Ann + Barney   Elissa
                                      Abrams   + Harvey
                                                    Steve
Jerry   Ethel   + Cecelia
  + Irene   + Lewis
Inez Lieberman   Leo + Ruth   Morton
Albert   Shulman   + Ina
  + Pearl   +   Alvin
Mike   Edna   + Jerry
  + Lieberman
Ellie   Sally + Al   Paul
                                      Bisno   Leslie
Bess Lampert
Rochelle Gordon   Ida + Sam Ellegant
                                    Libby + Albert Benjamin

                    Dinah
                + Harry Pershin —
Saralie   Bobbie   Beverly   Lenny
  +   +   +   +
Seymour   George   Bernard   Lois
Dolgin   Hammerman   Tanenbaum   Pershin

Betsy Ricki Miriam   Stuart Ken   Harold Myron Mikki   Laura Lisa
  +   Sternstein + Natalie + Sara Naomi   + Ken + Jeff
Michael Kate   Raynor Zeldes
       Jeff Amy   Michael   Andrea Marnie
Allen Hannah   Penny   Cara

ZAFTIG

In Russia, the winters were so cold,
Dinah sucked the marrow from chicken
Bones to keep meat on her own.
In America, she grew thin and pale,
Working in the factory long hours.
Harry's furrowed brow, his large hands
On her waist, his eyes at his feet
When he whispered—

Dinah, my love, you are turning into nothing.

We are a people of potatoes and
Onions, baking meatballs and knishes
Til they are soft as our mother's breasts,
Cholent and chicken fricassee,
A house is not a home without the smell
Of garlic turning brown over flame,
Without challah and blintzes and
Dunkers in black coffee, sipped slowly
While we sit around the table Remembering.

In Russia, Dinah slept on the stove
With her brothers and sisters,
Their toes warmed by baked bricks.
In America, she slept alone in a bed,
Next to her husband who she did not know.

Over the years she learned to love him,
Over the years she learned
The heart is a stove and
The body is a home.
Her hips spread like rising dough,
Her spine grew into cherry tree,
The root of us all—
The story we never stop telling.

GRANDY, 1939

Grandy 7 years old, digging through
dumpsters, pulling the final kernels
from already eaten corn. Excavating
the last sweetness from the rotten
plum. Beating the boys in the alley
with a broken high heel when they push
her fragile brother to the ground.

They want her poking breasts.
Her razortongue. Her rust.
They fear her like Tuberculosis
but hunger her nonetheless.
Fiend the fever.

Little girl Grandy making dolls of
Hollyhock blossoms from the alley,
turning them inside out, their cream
tongues twirling, long skirts. Wild
rosebush petals crushed by the wheel,

floating up to God in a puddle of mud.
She is pulling, pulling, placing them
delicate on her tiny fingertips like
long nails, pretending woman,
crushing them onto her cheeks,
blushed in her finding.

Great Depression baby, makeshift rouge, rogue
doily, ruffled sleeves smeared with sewage.
Crimson scrap, snuck silk. She cannot know
her body will one day be the arrow out of
the sling, dancing for soldiers, drunk hands
reaching, reaching, runway model strutting
catwalk at Somerset Mall. She cannot know

one day she will have a vanity wide and
white and turquoise as ocean: 4 drawers
just for her. Her lipstick, blush, mascara,
rings of opal and silver. Her mouth
a ruby set in olive skin. Her lipstick print-
her trademark. On envelopes, windows,
men. The red fades but the wax doesn't.
Her ghostlips for months after she's left.

I'll probably die from Red Dye #6.
My lipstick will be the end of me.
~ Grandy

A DRESSED UP POTATO IS STILL A POTATO (YIDDISH PROVERB)

i wear a dress
of potato peels, a
gown of garlic cloves,
sown by long winter women,
my hard-headed ancestors. i wear
their writhing roots across my scalp,
pulled from earth when they left in the
night, before krystalnacht. i wear shattered glass
in my gums, i wear their leaving like a long cloak,
like a heavy broach, child brides marrying first cousins
for green cards, tongues cut, sadstink from ship bottom
stuck in the fabric, i wear their gloomswallowed sundays,
their goldgiven fridays, shabbas candles hanging from earlobes,
chicken foot bracelets, evil eyes dangling over all of my days. i
wear their warnings & their worries, matreshkas for feet, hamsas
for hands. i see the news- more babies died in gaza this week
& all my layers shudder. necklace of swallowedsong tightening round
throat, i wear the dead ones too, the ones who didn't make it, in the hook
of my nose, stubborn curl at my temple that refuses to straighten, refuses
to pretend it is anything but itself. whiteness allowed my people to forget
where they came from. but as the elders like to say *a dressed up potato is still
a potato*. we all think we perform americana so well. but no matter how
glamorous my grandy is, her old country shines through, trips off
tongue when yiddish slips out & no one's left to translate her
memories. i wear her dead language as lipliner. all the ghosts
rattling my ribs, begging me not to forget. i wear our country's
ugly in my skin, in pale curve of hip that deems me more worthy
of protecting now. but cleansing then. nothing i wear is clean,
blood striped cotton, flag woven into wardrobe. i see the news-
more babies died in gaza this week & all my layers shudder.
i wear a shawl of prayers & it is not enough. i always read about
the germans who resisted, the woman who seduced nazis & then
killed them. who would have risked their life for me then? what am
i willing to give up now? i wear a dress of potato peels sown
by long winter women, i wear their terror & their chutzpa.
i wear the unborn ones too. how will we answer our
grandchildren when they ask: what did you do?
when they look at us & they are wearing our
faces, small mirrors, will i lace their necks
with swallowedsong? or will they pull this
shattered glass from their gums
& wield their words
like weapons?

For 85 years I've been a proud
Jew, and I'm pissed. I stand with
all people of color. Fuck Trump!
And nazis too.

~ Grandy, 2017

AT MY CENTER

My mom used to pinch my dad's butt
When she thought we weren't looking.

Summer nights in Muskegon,
I'd curl into my sister as she slept
Press my nose to her scalp full of sand.
It smelled like Lake Michigan,
Like my blood in another body.

In the kitchen, before school,
The sun would filter through the blinds
Onto our upturned faces, waiting
For Dad to sneak us a sugar cube
While his coffee warmed.

I would hold it between my teeth,
Sucking until the grains fell like stars.

This is how I move through life-

Holding that
Sweetness
At my center,
Like a secret
That will hurt
No one.

PREPARING FOR PESACH DURING A PANDEMIC

these days,

    i spend hours in our yellow kitchen

under bouquet of dried lavender,

      3 lemons in the hanging basket

          & the watchful eyes of my ancestors

they whisper to me

      when the pot whistles

sing me stories

      while the steam rises

            tell me again dinah,
            your first day in this new country

how you bit the banana, peel & all;

    how no one told you there was something sweet & soft beneath

i thought

    so this is america,
    this hard yellow thing

tell me again

          how in the old country, your father the tailor

stole silk from the inner lining of a rich lady's coat

    to swaddle your baby sister in

the day she was born

||

these days,

i spend hours stretched loose across our burgundy couch

beneath the charms & gifts that hold me:

melika's evil eye above our doorway -
blue sphere of glass slowly spinning

ceramic gift she brought me from morocco -
hand of fatima (for muslims)
hand of hamsa (for jews)

our people speak different languages but share the same symbols

i kiss the mezuzah jesmyn gave me
that welcomes me when i come home

and now i am home

always

welcome

always

alone

but safe

this hard yellow thing

passover approaches &

my mind tumbles: the plagues, the frogs, the locusts

i laugh   thinking of our makeshift seder plate: egg, bone, bitter herbs

hazarat: bright fuchsia horseradish that burned our eyes as children

ma nishtana: what makes this night different from all other nights?

our abridged haggadah we say in unison every year:

they tried to kill us
we survived
let's eat

|||

they say ashkenazi jews are more susceptible to illness

       trauma tangled veins

              i've always been a sick kid
              i've always been a blessed woman

my lungs are weak but
my blood is strong

              we survived   we survived   we survived

i am the matryoshka:

       the girl
       inside the mother
       inside the grandmother

              peel myself like banana &

                        i will find you again & again
dinya
    asna
        dinah
          fanny
             betty
                evie
                    freda
                       lois
                          laura

stealing silk from silver lining

protected, in my kitchen

unraveling yellow,

tasting the sweet & soft

beneath

II BRAIDING

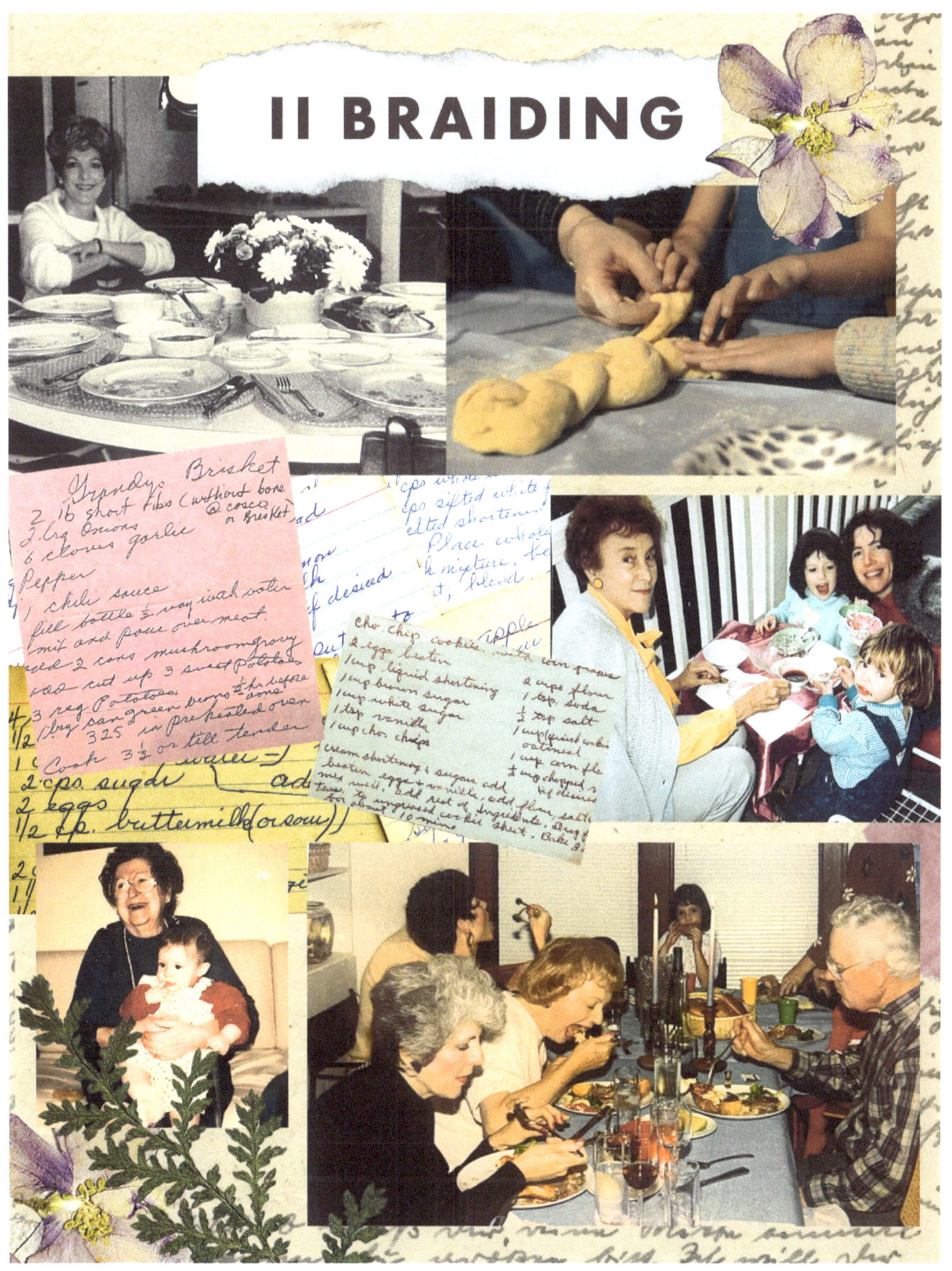

THIS IS THE UNDONE SEASON

of blunted grief, convenient beast.
Eyes heavy with tethered salt, veiled
sugar beneath silk swell of reddened
skin, conjured stink of yellowed shame.

Everything numbed under blanket
of ice, the dark confetti of your
absence: softshrapnel in my empty
bed. I black widow, weaving web

of what ifs & bloated regret, breasts
plump with ghostmilk of children
we named but never had. You were
a wishbone & me always breaking

off the smaller side. Trying to unearth
the dark pit of your distance, turn your
iron to velvet. I bluebird, threading
empty nest of eyelashes & dandelions,

so many midnight prayers that never
bore fruit. Still, they sing in me, pulsing
hot beneath this sorrow-studded shield.
This is the undone season of burrowing,

when all one can do is plant a seed &
pray it takes root. Praise this dumb
muscle that keeps beating, keeps
believing in spring. Praise this plump

miracle, purpledrunk with lilac blood.

FEIGELE

My Yiddish name is Feigele, which translates to "little bird" in English.
Feigele is now used as a derogatory slang word for queer people.

Even when she tries to write a poem to her boyfriend about the way he
Lifts her onto his bookshelf, rattling his faded science fiction to the floor,

Even when she feels weightless and powerless and so much a woman
Under him, above him, she knows that before him, and after him   she is Queer.

She was always a wild girl. Sucking on dandelions, then weaving them into crowns.
She wore those crowns but they never wore her: tomboy / boygirl / dirty knees / soccer star.

You would never guess from looking at her now-
She looks so straight. Straight enough that her elders believe she is;

Three years with J was a farce, a phase. She will marry a man and
Maybe he won't be Jewish but he will not be a woman, *puh puh puh.*

When she told her grandparents, Grandy recovered quickly-
Fuck men! Who needs them anyway? But Poppa turned red as the little birds

He loved to watch out his window, then called her a *whore* in Yiddish.
They don't speak of this anymore. She's sure they hope the phase has

Passed. Like Queer is something that passes, that dies without water,
Something to sit shiva for if anyone mourned its loss.

TOO MUCH [ZAFTIG II]

a love poem

I.

damn girl, look at those thick ass thighs.
& those titties, lord.

i regret my outfit / too much flesh /
skin billowing from my empty spots
til i tuck it all in / my glare: an exit
sign / still, they demand entrance /
i'm a winged thing /too heavy for
flight / satin insect stuck in resin
of their stare / these men / i   can't
breathe / the way they look at my
crotch / before they look at my face

what's wrong baby, why won't you smile for me?

your mouth: a temporary holding cell
/ but i'm more concerned with the
men behind your tongue / the silent
ones / who do not cat call / who
regulate through law / break treaties
like hymens, easy / my belly waxes
& wanes with tide / trying / to love
myself full / trying / trying / do you
not see my headphones? / cocoon of
jhené & bey thickening me / like flour
in curry / ballooning me with joy /
still, you stamp it out / thumb over
moon / i am trying to rock my grief
to sleep / still, you want me to smile   *for you*

why do you try on so many outfits each morning?

at summer camp the skinny girls
wore booty shorts / so i did too /
they were allowed to keep theirs
on / the director said mine were
inappropriate / said i had to   change

30

                                                         why are you so bent on disappearing?

the women in my family force
feed fierce & fire shots sweet
here, eat! eat! finish what's on your plate!
if you lose 10 pounds i'll take you shopping
they killed us off in russia / here
we cleanse ourselves / shrink our
old country hips /un - immigrant
until we   fit

                                                              why do you take the bribe?

i'm tired of having this body /
some days / i just want to walk
to the corner store in peace

II.

                                                        who are you without your fear?

in my tomorrowland
                              i am a rooted thing   heavier   harder to sway

        no need for flight   when i'm   all fight
all fire

                        thick as honey   smelling of   jasmine &   blood

            i turn men   to   water   with   one   look

smirk a shank
            i take up all the space
                                        make everyone uncomfortable / even drake
no diets
        no watching my weight

who are you without their shame?

i ursula

monsterqueen of

ocean & oyster   pearl & coral

tentacles   &   naked   breasts   spilling

over   every

surface

splayed across   my   golden sheets

starfish

suctioned   to   reef

owned   by no man   but the

sea

in my tomorrowland

i only smile

for me

what will you tell your children when they ask how you got so big?

i'll tell them that
i'd rather be   too much
than not enough.

I like me. ~ Grandy

YOU KNOW YOU'VE
GOT COVID BRAIN

when you realize your dress is inside out / take
it off to fix it / put it back on / & then realize
it's still inside out / when you text all your exes
try to fan an old flame / afraid a new ember may
stray to wildfire / too tender for tinder / too tired
for tending / when you unfurl / when furlough
makes you lazy / or maybe it's just the first time
you've stopped moving in 36 years long enough
to hear your own pulse / & the cicadas / & the
crickets trilling / & the refrigerating humming /
& the dryer tumbling your clothes gentle as a
lover might flip you without intent to hurt you /
when your chiropractor is the only one who's
touched you in 4 months / & he's old & you
can't see his face behind his mask / & it's not
sexual / it's just a need he's filling outside of the
need he's being paid to fill / & you arch against
his heavy hands like a hungry sky / a horizon that
can't be reached no matter how far you drive /
when you're starting to forget touch / names of
streets / days of the week / but you remember
the strange meat of your dreams / scraps of
purple / of her / & dogs attacking / when the
world becomes blur of smoke & storm / mask &
flag / a bouquet of bullets & names to be said /
shouted / grieved / engraved / remember shards
of childhood pressed like a pill beneath your
tongue / coming loose / when it's all coming
loose & you know you must surrender to the
hot blue night / listen to the song of your empty
house / your lush lonely / when you take your
self off & try to fix it / when you realize you're
still

       inside

             out

ON FLYING

inside my blood there are one thousand joyarrows :
sugarmarrow when i bite the bone : skin freckled

with thunderglitter : my whole body a mercymachine :
a meadow of miracle : a sunset of scabbedscar &

angelbruise : ruby to gold : gold to sea : so silvergreen :
so supermoon : so bent on breathing my littlebirdlungs :

so bent on flying my snakespine : my wildtoes : my
tiltedcervix : my jewslopenose : how many nights i

wished it away : all the wrongcurves : all the bitnails &
fathips : the flatfrizz & stillsick : all the asthma & allergies

& epilepsy & celiac & chronic fatigue & weak & weak
& freak : until i read frida's diary & saw her castcanvas

cut off : until i woke to my own pain's purpose. inside
my blood there are one thousand mis-fired neurons

& bursts of go(d) : the doctors got it wrong : my whole
body right : my whole body : the first day of   spring.

MOVING BACK TO THE CITY
WHERE I WAS FIRST RAPED

^^^^^^^^^^^^^^^^^^^^^^^^^^^^^^^^^^^

is a ready kind of battle.
is a map of puckered silence.
a quickened step, a sour sunset,
racing light as it slips to slit. watch

me slice
through these
streets like violent silk,
soft savage, keys between
my knuckles, lady scissorhands
ready to slash the sky to violet scraps.

i know
what lurks
in the dark &
in the day. alleyways:
convenient shortcuts for
some, traps for others, shattered
gold, ghouls glittering on every corner.

this city
a map of pink regret,
corpses of all the girls i know
with names of men marqueeing their
bodies, who can't go to certain clubs, stores

this city
a minefield of maybe,
of *what if he's there*, re-routing
coffee runs to avoid all the hims that
hummed liquored hymns cross our hips

how
we try to
forget but geography
doesn't, letters clang against our
temples like flags, marking all the graves.

^^^^^^^^^^^^^^^^^^^^^^^^^^^^^^^^^^

or maybe moving home is like this: a riot
of roses unfolding in my bath, sugar & lavender
from the farmer's market boiling on stovetop, making
syrup so strong you can't sour it, can't erase us, try & dam(n)
an ocean, the breast that keeps on feeding, try & cut a worm, the
body that tills the soil, we writhe & multiply, we recede & t s u n a m I

i drove to dexter yesterday.

                                     passed the house on campus where

           it   happened,

passed a field of sunflowers,

          each dark mouth singing my name,

            a chorus of self,

each lionmaned flower   waving me on,

         propelling me to the blueberry farm, where

                                          my sister & i

filled red pails to the brim with fathipped indigo

       &   snuck bites   &   went home   &   baked a blueberry pie

  for our grandy

         who is the fiercest silver, a pressed diamond burning in my mouth,

          i'm making a new map.

   renaming every street after   a girl who

                               chose

        to return,

my fingers stained

         with my sweet, not my blood.

III RISING

LAURA'S INCREDIBLE QUICHE

INGREDIENTS:

4 eggs
1 cup half & half
1 cup uncooked spinach
$\frac{1}{2}$ lb. sharp cheddar cheese
nutmeg, parmesan cheese
1 frozen deep dish pie crust
$\frac{1}{4}$ lb. ham or bacon (or corned beef)

INSTRUCTIONS:

Heat crust at 250° for 10 mins.
Preheat oven to 450°
Wash and dry spinach
Place spinach in bottom of crust
Top with ham & cheese. Set aside
Beat together eggs and half & half
Add salt and pepper
Pour over spinach, ham and crust
Sprinkle with nutmeg & parmesan cheese
Bake at 450° for 15 minutes
Lower to 350° for 30 minutes

GRANDY, 1990

Grandy, 58 years old. Makes Poppa
promise he'll stop giving money to the
Hasids from the local temple every year.
Tells him to put his tzedakah elsewhere,

those old Jews don't need it.

She should know better. Poppa the
trickster. Sneaks the raisins from
her Raisin Bran one by one until
she becomes enraged and calls the
company to complain. Poppa,

stubborn. Writes checks anyways, like
Grandy secretly switches out his ballot
with a democratic vote when mailing it in.

One Monday morning, Hasid comes to
collect his yearly check. Poppa creaks
door open silently, whispers to the man
in black. Grandy walks out wearing black
too- black bra and panties, nipples
peeking through lace like wide eyes.

Hasid sees Grandy through the
open door, gasps
                              oy vey!
Grandy sees Hasid,
screams
                    Jesus fucking Christ!

Hasid never comes back. Mezuzah
on the door hangs its head in shame.
Poppa laughs his slow lion roar,
shoulders shaking, cheeks taut with

her wild.
His wicked woman.
His holy blasphemy.

Marry a
mensch like
your Poppa.
Or don't get
married... and
just have lots
of sex.

~ Grandy

for mari & lauren

in the temple of your cracking laugh i bend / praise the way poetry penned us kin freshman year /when you borrowed my magenta pants & i wrote you a note after the slam / asking you to be my friend / how bold we were / how unbroken / open as summer windows

>>>

in our dingy ann arbor apartment we watched *sex and the city* & played egyptian ratscrew / scratching each other with acrylic nails / rhinestones glittering like nightsky / in our first apartment in oakland we watched *top model* / fridge full of faded poems / chorizo & avocado / kitchen walls stained red with mole from the day we smashed 16 peppers to paste with bittersweet chocolate & lard from frida's cookbook / proud / candles lit on spell-soaked altars / draped in gold & peacock feathers / we found faith / peeled off our skinny jeans / flung our bras across the room under the wise eyes of billie, badu & gwendolyn / ghosts of madwomen insulating our walls in winter / when the sun sunk we'd blast beyoncé & dig through each other's closets / line our eyes with black kohl / because friday night in oakland was like the first time a boy kissed me with his tongue / we'd head to lukas where we became other women / all ginger rum & slow wine & eyes like baited fishhooks / trying to reclaim that which was taken from us / we, our own best dreams

>>>

in the gospel of your gossip / in the pews of your pep talks i kneel / praise the way i am seen by you / so many secrets stitched into seams of our lips / hips thickening with each other's heartbreak / came home for holidays & parents wondered if we'd been eating too much when it's the weight of bearing witness women carry round our waists / you archivists of my darkest days / how you lifted the garland of grief / slit the sash of shame to shreds of laughter & *fuck him* & mint-laced hookah smoke curling up to god / the darksugar of your love candied me / so many times you saved me from myself

>>>

lil' wayne & alanis morissette echoing down the 1 / the sweat & shimmer of girlbodies unfurling / we made pilgrimage to ocean / greyed lip of froth & foam / made fort of sunbleached wood / carved our names into the sand beneath the setting sun / took a picture of mari dancing / body silhouetted against burnt bloodorange sky / dusky croon of gulls flocking above / then on a whim, went to a tattoo shop in la & inked that frozen moment into our wrists / three of her spread into us: bracelet of chosen blood / my madwomen, you gather me / my kindest mirrors / my sweetest marrow / you are the salvaged shine of this heavy country / the glory cake in my tattered mouth / you unsorry my tongue / ease the violence from my tired body

in the scripture of our group text i press palms together /
psalms of sisterchurch blooming from our fenty fuchsia lips /
you are the holiest thing i know

GRANDY, 2002

Grandy teaches my sister and I to shop
the way she taught my momma and aunt.
Her methods fine-tuned over years of modeling:

Keep the tags on honey,
Wear it tonight and return it tomorrow.

Grandy puts in work at TJ's, at Marshall's,
her arms an endless basket for our clearance
items. Clearance only on her dime. Red sticker
woman, high off that $3.99, anything under $10.
It's more about the deals than the clothes themselves.

No beige for sallow complexions.

Teaches us to try on 30 things and buy 3.
Who cares we take up 4 fitting rooms, not
Grandy. Shrill voice echoing off walls,
banging against the 3-way mirror:

If you've got it flaunt it, let your boobeles fly free!
Honey, you've got camel toe in those jeans- that's a no!

My sister and I roll eyes but never backtalk.
No convincing Grandy when it comes to fabric.
Fashion. Resale shops- her palace, we the lucky
peasants hugging our plastic bags, plump with
cheap halter tops and summer dresses.

If you don't love it, if you even have to question it, don't get it.

I think of Grandy while scrolling through
hundreds of Tinder profiles.

You gotta dig through all the shit to find the treasure!

I know what to look for,
The diamond on the
clearance rack. The
mensch in the ruff.

When I die, sprinkle my ashes across the top of TJ Maxx.
~ Grandy

APRIL 2020:
BRING ME WATER
FOR THESE FLOWERS
GROWING OUT MY MIND
~Badu

now cutflowers have become hard
to come by, a scarcity of tulips.

but the wildflowers are not scarce,
the wildflowers are unruly & plush,

magnolia tongues pushing pink
to the sky, swords of forsythia

slicing the air golden. april snow
falls soft & thick outside & i

am terrified that when it clears
the new buds will be frozen,

dead before they could live. but
tomorrow comes & there they

are. still alive. pale & pink &
trembling, fearless as they are

fragile. i dress up for no one but
my bought bouquets, coordinate

my outfit with magenta throat of
the daylilly, paint on grandma

evie's coral lipstick to match the
ruffled kiss of the ranunculus.

when the real flowers die, i take
instagram selfies with flower

filters, violet hibiscus sprouting
from my dimple, eclipsing my

worry lines. i am endless now,
a sea of lilacs, a perfumed body.

taking a masked walk with my mom &
grandy, i joke that i might sneak

out in the night & steal one of each
to make a garland, so hungry i am

for color, for scent, for the touch
of something else living in my home.

mom scolds me for even thinking
of such theft. but when we get

to the car, grandy whispers
across the distance between us:

steal the flowers, molly, just do it.
life is short & you deserve to smell

hyacinth every morning. grandy,
who just survived a stroke on

wednesday, smiles & winks &
drives away twinkling, my blood

blooming w   i   l   d
down the long, w i d e   street.

i wore a rosegold gown of smoke / palm fronds / murky water
swamp of want / moonflower / i open brightest in the velvet
knife of night / shadows sage every room in the palace of my
memory / mica & black sand / what slow erasure / what fear
we hold in our kidneys / my heart a fist cool & sturdy as jade /
i am 34 & 3 + 4 = 7 witch is my favorite number / this is my year
of pulling the knots loose / sewing momma's advice & smoky
quartz into the seams so i stay longer / i went to the arb on rosh
hashanah / wrote the names of all the men on coral leaves in black
sharpie & flushed them down the river / unraveled my blood of
them / i wrote all my names onto stone & buried it there beneath
tangled roots / ate cold apple slices dipped in honey / sticky on
my wrist / i licked it clean & felt shanklike & creamlike all at once
/ this alchemy of fear lifting like fog / shifting to freedom over
flame / rosegold smoke wrapping me in wedding gown / i met
myself beneath the chuppa / i met myself & said   *i do*

LABOR

of love. of tomatoes
softened in the oven,
puckered & oiled
with smoked salt.
i used to spend my
nights curled against
a warm body. now
i bake at 2am, now
i turn hard things
tender. turn cold
butter silken as her
neck. lean into the
dough like a new
job, like an old
song. it is always
350 degrees & the
garlic browns & the
bread rises sweet as
morning in the
windowsill, glazed
golden in yolk, a
singular segulah, &
i think i understand
now what slow means,
what waiting yields,
what harvest comes
from love, from labor.

ZAFTIG III

Dinah, my love,
you are turning into nothing.

Sometimes,

I want to file myself down to the bone,
Become small enough to be swept away.

But my body remembers its root and
I hug my hips like the children
They will someday carry.

In the end, I want to be something.

The kind of woman
Who sucks the marrow from bones,
Who sprouts cherries from her skull,

The kind of woman
Even a flood
Could not move.

WANT TO LISTEN ALONG?

Scan the QR code below and check out the Spotify album featuring selected poems from *ZAFTIG* read by Molly and set to music by world-renowned musician Josef Deas!

ACKNOWLEDGMENTS

Thank you to the following journals who previously published versions of these poems ~

"I COME FROM WOMEN WHO MADE LOVE WORK" in Calyx (2022)

"ZAFTIG" in *Love Me, Love My Belly*, PorkBelly Press (2017)

"A DRESSED UP POTATO IS STILL A POTATO" in Knight's Literary Magazine (2021)

"AT MY CENTER" in *Pure Volume: Poems by Coert Ambrosino, Molly Raynor & Adam Falkner,* Red Beard Press (2012)

"THIS IS THE UNDONE SEASON" in Terra Preta Review (2019)

"FEIGELE" in *Pure Volume: Poems by Coert Ambrosino, Molly Raynor & Adam Falkner*, Red Beard Press (2012)

"TOO MUCH" in *Love Me, Love My Belly*, PorkBelly Press (2017)

"YOU KNOW YOU'VE GOT COVID BRAIN" in Pedestal Magazine (2020)

"MOVING BACK TO THE CITY WHERE I WAS FIRST RAPED" in *Enough*, The Rumpus (2018)

"ON FLYING" in *Issue 7,* Sugared Water Magazine, Porkbelly Press (2022)

"GRANDY, 1990" honorable mention in the 2017 Anna Davidson Rosenberg Poetry Awards, Poetica Publishing (2017)

"SISTERCHURCH" in *Tattoosday*, The Tattooed Poets Project (2018)

"APRIL 2020: BRING ME WATER FOR THESE FLOWERS GROWING OUT MY MIND" forthcoming in *Issue #2*, Public School Poetry (2024)

"YAMIM NORAIM /// DAYS OF AWE" in Terra Preta Review (2019)

"LABOR" in *In Absentia: Reflections on the Pandemic,* Bicycle Comics (2020)

GRATITUDE

I am so grateful to Fifth Avenue Press for publishing *ZAFTIG*- it feels so full circle to find a home for my book at the Ann Arbor District Library which was always my second home growing up. In particular, thank you to Erin Helmrich for believing in my book and offering endless support, to Nate Pocsi-Morrison for designing the book so beautifully, to Zilka Joseph for your wonderful edits and suggestions, and to Cameron Finch for your guidance with marketing. To Josef Deas for creating beautiful music to go with my poetry for the recorded album and live release- I feel beyond blessed for this collaboration after admiring your music since we were teens. And to Thea Eck at the Ann Arbor Art Center for hosting my book release.

Thank you to my family of storytellers and tricksters, particularly my seester bird Emma, my daddy-o Ken, and my mamele Laura whose devotion to stories led me to fall in love with language from a young age. To Jason, Lauren, Danny, Meghan, Lisa, Jeff, Onna, Jonathan, Gabe, Lisa, Linda, Rick, Ina, Rob, Lily, Izzy, Abby, Nick, Terri, Jo, Fred, Austin, Marc, Amy, Cindy, Denny, Jojo, Kylie, Paula, Julie, Larry, Barb and the rest of my amazing family. And obviously Grandy. Forever Grandy.

Thank you to my most impactful mentor, Jeff Kass, who saw something in me at 14 that I couldn't yet see and has helped me shine ever since.

To my madwomen—Lauren Whitehead and Mariama Lockington—and to my dear friends Yalie Saweda Kamara, José Vadi and Liz Latty, who hold me accountable to my writing dreams #thegroupworks.

To my bosom friends, my "kindest mirrors"- Ariel Lewiton, Carla Joy Thomas McGinnis, Kelsey Cavanagh-Strong, CieraJevae Gordon, Ross Harris & Kai's siblings, Reed Swier, Nate Broyles, Melika Belhaj, Carlina Duan, Erin & Jameson Wolf, Kristen and Matt DeLeon-Hamilton, Katie Milne, Angel Nafis, Shira Erlichman, Sara Abelson, Kate Benham, Matt Hunter, Day Washington, Marlin M. Jenkins, Jen Haines, Ike Nwankwo, Tre McClure, Nikki D'Angelo, Molly Nestor, Hannah Deschaine, Sarah Kurtz, Jordan Peshke, Coert Ambrosino, Maggie Ambrosino, Sadie Yarrington, Alia Persico-Shammas, Johnny Floyd, Brittany Floyd, MARS Marshall, Devin Samuels, Donté Clark, Nyabingha Zianni McDowell, Deandre Evans, D'Neise Robinson, Nia Snipes, Jamaya Walker, Micah Brumfield, TJ Sykes, George Mitchell, Marjé Kilpatrick, Kawah, Paris Slaton, DiMarea Young, Angela Miller-Robinson, Dylan Gilbert, Ciatta Tucker, Venus Pasha, Naima Peterson, Malik Henry, Maria Theocharakis, Sakinah & Zakiyyah Rahman, Shane Collins, Ashanti Kenyatta Campbell, Samuel Martin, Anika Love, Jason Williams, Kyndall Flowers, Lilly Kujawski, Zaphra Stupple, Aldo Leopoldo Pando Girard, Hasna Ghalib, Julianna Morano, Jesmyn Ward, Alma Davila-Toro, Ash Arder, Lisandra and Natasha Fernandez-Silber, Ana Agüero Jahannes, Suhaley Bautista-Carolina, Karaline Zeigler, Diana Turner, Claire Forster, Jamall Bufford, Lisa Dengiz, Anya Black, Max Gibson, Raynell Crews-Gamez, Marilyn Hollinquest, Brooke Wilson, Kyla Danysh, Stacy Daniels, Gabriel Cortez, Natasha Huey, Alex Alaniz, Noran Alsabahi, Anjali Rodrigues, Farima Pour-Khorshid, Kush Thompson, Felicia Hasal, Heather Martin, Desiraé Simmons, Noah Arhm Choi, Adam Falkner, Jonah Thompson, Michelle Mush Lee, Brittany and Justin Rogers, Ajanaé Dawkins, Sonya Renee Taylor, Tracey Samone Clark, Rachel Van Parys, Monique LeBlanc-

Qureshi, LeShea Newton, Hassan Hassan, Alyse Nicholson, Lydia Mercer, Laura Dominguez, LaShaune Stitt, Brandy Williams, Jen Chiou, Norma Velasquez, Joan Jungbin Lee, Nyesha Trusty, Keaton Wadzinski, Chelsea Nieman, Jaclyn Remick, Amy Waters, Daniel Bigham, Chavonna Bigham, Ryan Dorsey, Courtney Whittler, Jonathan Desir, Sonya Carter, Eli and Penny Marienthal, Vanessa Holden, Fiona Chamness, Faye Askew-King, Bri Luna, Kiese Laymon, Rosa Cabrera, Ellen Stone, Dawn Espy, Lauren Fardig-Diop, Becca Wright, Gina Thompson, Amanda Gurny, Kristyn Driver, Sandy Ryder, the Lewiton Lown family, the Schneider family, the Solomon-Iglesias family, & Andrea, Lily & Phoebe Rachles.

To the communities that have taught me, held me, pushed me to be my best self- especially my RAW Talent/Making Waves/RYSE/Richmond family, my Staying Power squad, my In Surreal Life community of weirdos and wordsmiths, and beloveds I met through The Eddy Line, AGQ, Volume, WordWorks, BNV and 4.0 Schools— there are too many of you to name but you know who you are and how much I love you. To the JCC where I grew up and the radical, witchy, antizionist Jewish communities that have helped me root into my culture and faith- the Kohenet Hebrew Priestess Institute, Jewish Voice for Peace and Dreaming the World to Come. To the cities that have shaped me most: Ann Arbor, Ypsilanti, Detroit, Oakland, Richmond and New Orleans. To the brave intersectional feminists of past and present who inform my politics and inspire my art. To my ancestors. I am forever grateful for this gleaming life of mine.

Special shout out to my mom, Emma, Marlin, Mariama and Cozine Welch Jr. who helped me edit this collection. And again to Yalie, Carlina, Shira and Kush for your care, attention and celebration of my work.

Finally, thank you to my son Malachi Moon, my lunar light, my little miracle. I started this book when you were just a dream, but I finished it once I knew you were growing inside me- I had always wanted to create a body of work before I created a body. As I near "midlife" and enter this new phase of motherhood, I have been reflecting on my role as a descendant and the transition towards becoming an ancestor. What legacy will I leave for my child, possible grandchildren, great grandchildren? I want to use the next half of my life to heal generational trauma and archive our ancestral resilience, creating artifacts like this one to pass down.

LAND & LABOR ACKNOWLEDGMENT

The first part of this acknowledgment was written in collaboration with CieraJevae Gordon, Dawn Espy and Cheyenne Travioli for our 2022 Staying Power production.

Let us first begin by acknowledging that we are on stolen land. It is crucial to speak of our Indigenous community in present tense. They are still here, and still fighting amongst us, as we are here fighting with them. Today we plant a seed in the ground that will grow and nurture its roots in the land of the Anishinabewaki, the Fox, the Peoria, and the Potawatomi.

As we acknowledge the Indigenous peoples who have — and continue to — live here, steward this land, and resist settler colonialism, we also acknowledge that this country has been built on the forced labor of African people through violent, systematic abduction from their homelands and enslavement over hundreds of years. We acknowledge the impacts this has had on African descendants through this country's development. We uplift, and honor those ancestors for their fight, their love, and their legacies.

We plant this seed knowing that the city lines do not define it, that the lines are a creation of man, not the creator. A false claim to property which was not theirs to parse. We honor not only our past but our present and future. In our present we lift up those actively fighting—the water protectors, the climate justice warriors, those that have existed on the boundaries and margins because their voice has been silenced and their land has been co-opted. We celebrate those who are trying to save us all, despite our continued decimation of the land. We lift up climate justice as our land begs for help. Let those who have stewarded this land for centuries guide us.

~

Finally, I honor Indigenous Palestinians who have been and continue to be forcibly removed from their homeland, murdered, assaulted and ethnically cleansed by the Israeli government and military in the name of Jewish people. As I put forth this very Jewish book into the world, I want to be abundantly clear where I stand: in solidarity with Palestinians. I stand against genocide. I stand against Zionism. I am rooted in the Jewish value of tikkun olam (repairing a broken world) and the prophetic tradition; I was raised to speak out against injustice, even when it's my own people perpetuating the very oppression we once faced. I am listening to my ancestors who said *never again*, to the "kitchen poets" who braided lessons into the bread and handed down recipes of resilience, not revenge.

Verbal acknowledgements are important but without action they are often just performative and must be backed up with action. In the Jewish tradition, the act of tzedakah (donating, reparations, etc.) is one such action. 20% of proceeds from this book will be go towards mutual aid efforts on the ground in Palestine, towards Indigenous land taxes, and towards organizations supporting decolonization and liberation in the US, Sudan, the Congo, Haiti and all other places where folks are facing oppression.

As Nina Simone said, "an artist's duty, as far as I'm concerned, is to reflect the times." May all of our art move us towards collective liberation.

ABOUT THE AUTHOR

MOLLY ZIPORA PERSHIN FEIGELE RAYNOR (she/her/hers) is a poet, educator, community builder and momma to Malachi Moon. Her poetry has been featured on NPR and published in several literary magazines including *Vinyl*, *The Rumpus*, *Porkbelly Press* and *Split Lip Magazine*.

Molly co-founded "RAW Talent" with Donté Clark, now the RYSE Center's Performing Arts Program, which serves youth in Richmond, California. Her work is highlighted in the documentary film, "Romeo Is Bleeding" which was on Netflix. Molly won a Jefferson Award for Public Service and a Teachers 4 Social Justice Award for her work in the Bay Area. In 2017, Molly moved home to Michigan where she received her Masters in Social Work from Eastern Michigan University, and co-founded "Staying Power," a youth arts activism program in Ypsilanti (inspired by the Staying Power collective in Richmond, CA.) She is currently the Director of Community at 4.0 Schools.

Molly draws inspiration from Audre Lorde, Octavia Butler, Robin Wall Kimmerer, Frida Kahlo, Paulo Freire and from the recipes, jokes and legacy of her ancestors. She comes from a long line of storytellers and plumbers who taught her how to bend words and weld new worlds.